JANICE VANCLEAVE'S
WILD, WACKY, AND WEIRD
SCIENCE EXPERIMENTS

MORE OF JANICE VANCLEAVE'S WILD, WACKY, AND WEIRD EARTH SCIENCE EXPERIMENTS

Illustrations by
Lorna William

ROSEN
PUBLISHING

NEW YORK

This edition published in 2017 by
The Rosen Publishing Group, Inc.
29 East 21st Street
New York, NY 10010

Library of Congress Cataloging-in-Publication Data

Names: VanCleave, Janice.
Title: More of Janice VanCleave's wild, wacky, and weird earth science experiments / Janice VanCleave.
Description: New York : Rosen YA, 2017. | Series: Janice Vancleave's wild, wacky, and weird science experiments | Includes index.
Identifiers: LCCN ISBN 9781499465495 (pbk.) | ISBN 9781499465518 (library bound) | ISBN 9781499465501 (6-pack)
Subjects: LCSH: Earth sciences—Experiments—Juvenile literature.
Classification: LCC QE29.V364 2016 | DDC 550.78—dc23

Manufactured in the United States of America

Illustrations by Lorna William

Experiments first published in *Janice VanCleave's 202* Oozing, Bubbling, Dripping, and *Bouncing Experiments* by John Wiley & Sons, Inc. copyright © 1996 Janice VanCleave and *Janice VanCleave's 200 Gooey, Slippery, Slimy, Weird and Fun Experiment*s by John Wiley & Sons, Inc. copyright © 1992 Janice VanCleave.

CONTENTS

Introduction 4

Fill It Up 8

Downdraft 10

Updraft 12

Sea Breezes 14

Block Out 16

Rain Gauge 18

Under Cover 20

Twister 22

Boom! 24

Waves 26

Sinker 28

Weight Loss 30

What's Up 32

Tasty 34

Salty Water 36

Tides 38

Clean Up 40

Floater 42

Bulging Ball 44

Precession 46

Wobbler 48

Day and Night 50

Twilight 52

Salty 54

Glossary 56

For More Information 58

For Further Reading 61

Index 63

INTRODUCTION

Earth science is the field of study that deals with planet Earth. Geology is one main area of earth science that looks at the physical planet. But oceanography, meteorology, and astronomy are also areas of earth science.

The people who decide to work in the field of earth science have a variety of career paths to choose from. Some work in laboratories. Others work outdoors and study soil, fossils, volcanoes, and earthquakes. All of these people have something in common: They are constantly asking questions to learn even more about our planet.

This book is a collection of science experiments about earth science. Why isn't the sky dark immediately after sunset? What causes sea breezes? What makes thunder? You will find the answers to these and many other questions by doing the experiments in this book.

HOW TO USE THIS BOOK

You will be rewarded with successful experiments if you read each experiment carefully, follow the steps in order, and do not substitute materials. The following sections are included for all the experiments.

» **PURPOSE:** *The basic goals for the experiment.*

» **MATERIALS:** *A list of supplies you will need.* You will experience less frustration and more fun if you gather all the necessary materials for the experiments before you begin. You lose your train of thought when you have to stop and search for supplies.

» **PROCEDURE:** *Step-by-step instructions on how to perform the experiment.* Follow each step very carefully, never skip steps, and do not add your own. Safety is of the utmost importance, and by reading the experiment before starting, then following the instructions exactly, you can feel confident that no unexpected results will occur. Ask an adult to help you when you are working with anything sharp or hot. If adult supervision is required, it will be noted in the experiment.

» **RESULTS:** *An explanation stating exactly what is expected to happen.* This is an immediate learning tool. If the expected results are achieved, you will know that you did the experiment correctly. If your results are not the same as described in the experiment, carefully read the instructions and start over from the first step.

» **WHY?** *An explanation of why the results were achieved.*

INTRODUCTION

THE SCIENTIFIC METHOD

Scientists identify a problem or observe an event. Then they seek solutions or explanations through research and experimentation. By doing the experiments in this book, you will learn to follow experimental steps and make observations. You will also learn many scientific principles that have to do with earth science.

In the process, the things you see or learn may lead you to new questions. For example, perhaps you have completed the experiment that investigates whether water pressure is affected by volume. Now you wonder whether water pressure is affected by temperature. That's great! All scientists are curious and ask new questions about what they learn. When you design a new experiment, it is a good idea to follow the scientific method.

1. Ask a question.

2. Do some research about your question. What do you already know?

3. Come up with a hypothesis, or a possible answer to your question.

4. Design an experiment to test your hypothesis. Make sure the experiment is repeatable.

5. Collect the data and make observations.

6. Analyze your results.

7. Reach a conclusion. Did your results support your hypothesis?

Many times the experiment leads to more questions and a new experiment.

Always remember that when devising your own science experiment, have a knowledgeable adult review it with you before trying it out. Ask them to supervise it as well.

FILL IT UP

PURPOSE To demonstrate that air takes up space.

MATERIALS large bowl, deeper than the height of the plastic
drinking glasses
tap water
masking tape
marking pen
two 7-ounce (210-ml) clear plastic drinking glasses

PROCEDURE

1. Fill the bowl about three-fourths full with water.

2. Use the tape and marking pen to label the glasses A and B.

3. Put glass A into the water on its side, so that it fills up with water.

4. Turn the filled glass A upside down in the bowl.

5. Hold glass B upside down above the water and, keeping it straight, push it completely under the water.

6. Move glasses A and B together and slightly tilt their mouths toward each other. The edge of glass B should be under the rim of glass A, so that the bubbles from glass B rise into glass A.

RESULTS Glass A fills with air and glass B fills with water.

WHY? When glass B is pushed into the water, the air inside the glass prevents the water from entering the glass. Bubbles of air from glass B

8

rise in the water because air is lighter than water. The rising air bubbles push the water out and fill glass A. Water moves into glass B to take up the space that was occupied by the air.

DOWNDRAFT

PURPOSE To observe the effect of cool temperature on air movement.

MATERIALS drawing compass
tissue paper
scissors
transparent tape
12-inch (30-cm) piece of thread

PROCEDURE

1. Use the compass to draw a 3-inch (7.5-cm) circle on the tissue paper.

2. Cut the circle into a spiral as shown.

3. Tape one end of the thread to the center of the paper spiral.

4. Open the refrigerator door about 8 inches (20 cm).

5. Holding the free end of the thread, hold the paper spiral just inside the bottom of the door opening.

NOTE: Keep the spiral from this activity for the next experiment.

RESULTS The paper spiral twirls.

WHY? Cold air molecules have less energy and move around more slowly than do more energetic warm air molecules. The slow-moving cold air molecules tend not to move away from each other. Therefore, cold air, with its slow molecules spaced close together, is heavier than warm air, with its speedy molecules spread apart. This causes colder, heavier air to sink, and warmer, lighter air to rise. Sinking air is called a downdraft and rising air is called an updraft. The downdraft from the refrigerator hits the spiral, causing it to turn.

UPDRAFT

PURPOSE To determine the effect of warm temperature on air movement.

MATERIALS spiral from previous experiment
package of instant hot chocolate
coffee mug
1 cup (250 ml) tap water
spoon
adult helper

PROCEDURE

1. Ask an adult to prepare a cup of hot chocolate.

2. Hold the end of the thread and position the bottom of the paper spiral about 2 inches (5 cm) above the cup of hot chocolate.

RESULTS The paper spiral twirls.

WHY? The energy from the hot drink heats the air above it. The air molecules directly above the cup move faster and farther apart as they absorb energy. The separation of the molecules makes the air lighter and it rises upward. This upward movement of air is called an updraft. The updraft hits the spiral and causes it to twirl.

SEA BREEZES

PURPOSE To determine the cause of sea breezes.

MATERIALS ruler
tap water
2 glasses, large enough to hold the thermometers
soil
2 thermometers
timer
desk lamp

PROCEDURE

1. Pour 2 inches (5 cm) of water into the first glass.

2. Pour 2 inches (5 cm) of soil into the second glass.

3. Place a thermometer in each glass.

4. Set the glasses together on a table. Allow them to stand for 30 minutes before recording the reading on each thermometer.

5. Position the lamp so that the light evenly hits both glasses.

6. After 1 hour, turn the lamp off and compare the temperatures on the thermometers.

RESULTS The temperature of the soil is higher than the temperature of the water.

WHY? It takes more heat energy to change the temperature of the water. Thus, the water heats more slowly than the soil does. The difference in the time it takes for land and water to change temperature affects the movement of air above them. During the day, the land heats more quickly than the ocean. Warmer air above the land rises, and cooler air above the water rushes in to take the place of the rising warm air. This air movement is called a sea breeze.

Block Out

PURPOSE To determine how volcanic clouds can lower atmospheric temperature.

MATERIALS white poster board
ruler
clear plastic report cover
8 paper cups
cardboard, the size of the report cover
2 thermometers
timer

PROCEDURE

1. At midday on a sunny day, lay the poster board on a table outdoors or on the ground.

2. Set the paper cups, upside down, on the poster board. Space them so that one cup sits under each corner of the plastic sheet and cardboard, as shown.

3. Read and record the temperature on both thermometers. Then place one thermometer under each cover.

4. After 15 minutes, read the thermometer again.

RESULTS The thermometer under the clear plastic sheet has the higher temperature.

WHY? The clear plastic sheet is transparent, which means it allows light to pass through. The cardboard does not allow light to pass through, making it an opaque object. Normally, Earth's atmosphere is relatively transparent. The clouds formed by some volcanic eruptions contain opaque ash particles that block out some of the sun's solar rays. This results in a lowering of atmospheric temperature, just as the opaque cardboard blocking the sun's rays resulted in a lower temperature on the thermometer underneath it.

RAIN GAUGE

PURPOSE To make and use a rain gauge.

MATERIALS scissors
ruler
2-liter soda bottle
transparent tape
1 cup (250 ml) aquarium gravel or small rocks
tap water
adult helper

PROCEDURE

1. Ask an adult to cut the top off the bottle so that 8 inches (20 cm) remain. Discard the top.

2. Tape the ruler vertically to the side of the bottle with the zero end of the ruler at the bottom, just above the bottle's plastic base, as shown in the diagram.

3. Pour the gravel into the bottle. Then, pour water into the bottle until it reaches the zero end of the ruler.

4. Set the bottle in the corner of your shower stall or bathtub before you take a shower, or outside during a rainy day.

5. After you finish your shower or the rain has stopped, see how high the water is in the bottle.

RESULTS The height of the water depends on the amount of shower water or rain that fell.

WHY? The bottle with the ruler attached is a rain gauge. A rain gauge is an instrument that can be used to collect falling water. It measures the depth of water that would cover the ground or surface if none of the water drained away or evaporated. The gravel in the bottle weighs down the bottle so that it won't fall over. The water is added so that the water line begins at the zero end on the ruler.

UNDER COVER

PURPOSE To determine the effect of overhead covering on dew formation.

MATERIALS umbrella
2 sheets of black construction paper
timer

PROCEDURE

NOTE: Perform this experiment on several calm, clear nights during different seasons.

1. Just before sunset, open the umbrella and place it on the ground, as shown in the diagram.

2. Lay one sheet of paper under the umbrella and lay the other sheet of paper on the ground with no overhead covering.

3. After sunset, check the papers every 30 minutes for 2 hours.

RESULTS Water collects on the paper with no overhead covering, but not on the protected paper.

WHY? Dew point is the temperature at which dew forms. Dew is the water droplets that form when moisture in the air condenses (changes to liquid). The black paper cools by losing heat energy. The heat radiates (moves away) from the sheets of paper. The uncovered sheet loses enough energy to cool to dew point, so water condenses on its surface. Some of the heat from the covered paper is absorbed by the umbrella and is radiated back to the paper, keeping the paper from cooling to dew point. Clouds, tree branches, and other overhead coverings, like the umbrella, can prevent dew from forming on objects beneath them.

TWISTER

PURPOSE To demonstrate the shape of a tornado.

MATERIALS two 2-liter soda bottles
tap water
paper towel
flat metal washer with the same circumference as the
mouth of the bottles
duct tape
adult helper

PROCEDURE

1. Ask an adult to remove the plastic rings left on the necks of the bottles when the caps are removed.

2. Fill one bottle halfway with water.

3. Dry the mouth of the bottle with the paper towel and place the washer over the mouth of the bottle.

4. Place the second bottle upside down on top of the washer.

5. Secure the bottles together with tape.

6. Turn the bottles upside down so that the bottle with the water is on top. Stand the bottles on a table.

7. Place one hand around the lower bottle and the other hand on top of the upper bottle.

8. Support the lower bottle while quickly moving the top of the upper bottle in a small counterclockwise circle.

9. Stand the bottles upright, with the empty bottle remaining on the bottom.

RESULTS The water inside the upper bottle swirls in a counterclockwise direction, forming a funnel shape as it pours into the lower bottle.

WHY? The funnel formed by the swirling water is called a vortex (a whirling mass of air or water). The vortex formed in the water is the same shape as the vortex formed by a tornado (a violently rotating funnel cloud that touches the ground). A tornado looks like a swirling funnel hanging down from a dark thundercloud.

23

Boom!

PURPOSE To determine what causes thunder.

MATERIALS 9-inch (23-cm) round balloon
glove
straight pin

PROCEDURE

1. Inflate the balloon and make a knot.

2. Lay the inflated balloon on a table.

3. Place the glove on one hand.

4. Hold the pin with the gloved hand.

5. Stand at arm's length from the balloon.

6. Stick the pin into the balloon.

RESULTS When the pin is inserted into the balloon, the balloon rips. At the same time a loud popping noise is heard.

WHY? When your lungs force air inside the balloon, the rubber stretches and the balloon inflates. The air inside the balloon pushes outward. The stretched rubber pushes the air inside the balloon. Sticking the pin into the balloon makes a tiny tear. The stretched rubber immediately starts to pull at the tear. At the same time, the compressed air rushes out and pushes on the tear. The balloon breaks apart. As the compressed air rushes through the tear, it expands (moves apart). This quick expansion of air pushes outward against the air surrounding the balloon. This creates sound waves that reach your ears as a popping sound. Thunder is produced in a similar way. As lightning strikes, it gives off energy that heats the air through which it passes. This heated air quickly expands, then cools and contracts. The fast expansion and contraction of air around lightning causes air molecules to move back and forth, which in turn produces sound waves that you hear as thunder.

Boom!

WAVES

PURPOSE To demonstrate the motion of water waves.

MATERIALS Slinky toy
helper

PROCEDURE

1. Lay the Slinky on the floor.

2. Stretch the Slinky between you and your helper.

3. Gently move one end of the Slinky back and forth several times.

4. Change the speed of your back-and-forth movement by increasing and decreasing the distance the Slinky is moved.

RESULTS Waves of motion move from one end of the Slinky to the other. The wave size increases with an increase in the distance that the end is moved.

WHY? Waves that move up and down are called transverse waves. The highest part of each wave is called the crest, and the lowest part is called the trough. The movement of the Slinky is a flat version of how water waves look and move from one point to another. Waves move from one end of the Slinky to the other, but the material in the Slinky stays in relatively the same place. Water molecules, like the rings in the Slinky, move up and down, but they do not move forward. Only the energy of each wave moves forward.

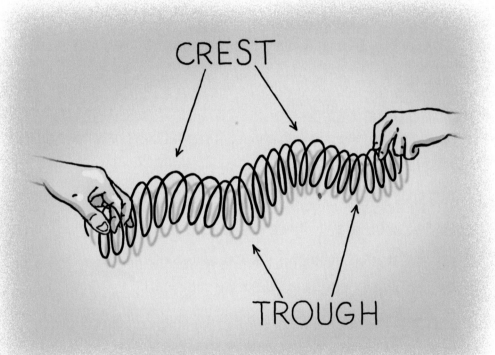

CREST

TROUGH

SINKER

PURPOSE To determine how density affects water movement.

MATERIALS 1-cup (250-ml) measuring cup
tap water
1/3 cup table salt
spoon
blue food coloring
2-quart (2-liter) glass container
helper

PROCEDURE

1. Fill the measuring cup with about 3/4 cup (200 ml) of water. Add the salt to the water and stir.

2. Add enough food coloring to make the water a very deep blue color.

3. Fill the container halfway with water.

4. Observe the container from the side as your helper slowly pours the blue salty water down the side of the container.

RESULTS The colored water sinks to the bottom of the container, forming waves under the clear water above it.

WHY? A density current is the movement of water due to the difference in the density of water. All sea water contains salt, but when two bodies of water mix, denser water (the water with the most salt) will move under the less dense water (the water with less salt).

More of Janice VanCleave's Wild, Wacky, and Weird Earth Science Experiments

WEIGHT LOSS

PURPOSE To demonstrate how density affects the ability to float.

MATERIALS 2-liter soda bottle with cap
tap water
glass eyedropper

PROCEDURE

1. Over a sink, completely fill the bottle with water.

2. Partially fill the eyedropper with water.

3. Drop the eyedropper into the bottle of water. If the eyedropper sinks, remove it, squeeze some of the water out, and drop it back in.

4. Be sure the bottle is full of water, then secure the cap on the bottle.

5. Squeeze the sides of the bottle with your hands.

6. Observe the eyedropper and the water level inside.

7. Release the bottle and observe the movement of the eyedropper and the water level inside.

RESULTS Squeezing causes the water to rise inside the eyedropper, and it sinks. When the bottle is released, the water level lowers inside the eyedropper, and the eyedropper moves upward.

WHY? Squeezing the bottle increases the pressure inside, causing water to move into the open eyedropper. The extra water increases the density of the eyedropper. It sinks because the upward push of the water is not great enough to hold up the now-heavier eyedropper. The dropper rises when its density is lessened by the loss of water. Submarines, like the dropper, move up and down in the water due to changes in density. The submarine sinks by taking water into side tanks and rises by blowing that water out.

WHAT'S UP

PURPOSE To determine if water pressure is affected by volume.

MATERIALS

2 sheets of newspaper
marking pen
ruler
paper cup, at least 4 inches (9 cm) tall
1-gallon (4-liter) plastic jug

large nail
masking tape
tap water
adult helper

PROCEDURE

1. Place both sheets of newspaper on the edge of a table outside.

2. Make one mark in the center of each sheet of paper.

3. Measure and mark heights of 1 inch (2.5 cm) and 3 inches (7.5 cm) on the cup and plastic jug.

4. Ask an adult to use the nail to punch a hole in the cup and the jug on the 1-inch (2.5-cm) mark.

5. Cover each hole with tape.

6. Fill each container with water to the 3-inch (7.5-cm) mark.

7. Place the papers side by side and set the edge of each container on the marks in the center of each sheet, with their holes facing in the same direction.

8. Remove the tape from each container.

RESULTS Water sprays out the same distance from each container.

WHY? The pressure of the water is due to its depth and not to the total volume of the water. Water pressure at a depth of 2 yards (2 m) is the same in a swimming pool as it would be in the ocean. The pressure of the water is due to the amount of water pushing down. Water pressure increases with depth, due to more water pushing down from above.

TASTY

PURPOSE To determine the taste of ocean water.

MATERIALS two 9-ounce (180-ml) cups
tap water
1/4 teaspoon (0.63 ml) table salt
spoon
marking pen

NOTE: Never taste anything in a laboratory setting unless you are sure that it does not contain chemicals or materials.

PROCEDURE

1. Fill each cup halfway with water.

2. Add the salt to one of the cups of water and stir.

3. Label the cup containing the salt S.

4. Taste the water in each cup.

RESULTS The cup marked S tastes salty.

WHY? Ocean water, like the water in cup S, tastes salty because of the salt dissolved in it. A mixture of 1/4 teaspoon (0.63 ml) of table salt in 90 ml of water contains about the same amount of salt as ocean water does. Sodium chloride is the chemical name for table salt, which is the most abundant salt in seawater.

Salty Water

Purpose To determine how the ocean gets its salt.

Materials

pencil

2 paper cups

coffee filter

1 tablespoon (15 ml) soil

1 tablespoon (15 ml) table salt

spoon

sheet of black construction paper

plate

modeling clay

tap water

Procedure

1. Use the pencil to punch 6 holes in the bottom of one of the paper cups.

2. Place the coffee filter inside the cup.

3. In the other cup, mix the soil and the salt together.

4. Pour the soil-salt mixture into the cup with the coffee filter.

5. Place the paper on the plate.

6. Use the clay to make short legs to support the cup above the paper.

7. Add spoonfuls of water until water starts to drain out of the cup.

8. Allow the water to drain. Then let the paper dry.

Results White crystals of salt form on the paper.

WHY? As the water flows through the soil, the salt dissolves in it and collects on the black paper. As the water evaporates from the paper, the dry salt is left behind. In nature, rainwater dissolves salt from the soil. If this water finds its way to rivers that flow into the ocean, the salt is added to the ocean water.

TIDES

PURPOSE To determine the effect of centrifugal force on tides.

MATERIALS pencil
7-ounce (210-ml) paper cup
24-inch (60-cm) piece of string
tap water

PROCEDURE

1. Use the pencil to punch 2 holes across from each other beneath the top rim of the paper cup.

2. Tie the ends of the string through each hole in the cup.

3. Fill the cup one-fourth full with water.

4. Take the cup outside.

5. Hold the string and swing the cup around in a horizontal circle above your head several times.

RESULTS The cup turns sideways, but the water stays inside the spinning cup.

WHY? The gravitational pull of the moon causes the ocean water to bulge on the side of Earth facing the moon. There is another bulge of water on the side of Earth opposite the moon. This second bulge results partly from the rotation of Earth. Spinning produces a centrifugal force that causes the turning object to tend to fly away from the center around which it turns. The water in the cup moves outward because of centrifugal force, but the paper cup prevents it from flying away. The revolution of

Earth around the sun produces a centrifugal force. Earth's rotation about its own axis contributes to this force. The result of this spinning, as well as of the position of the moon and sun, is a bulging of the ocean waters on Earth, called high tides. The bulging water is prevented from spinning out into space by Earth's gravitational force.

EARTH

MOON

CLEAN UP

PURPOSE To demonstrate a way to clean up an oil slick.

MATERIALS clear drinking glass
tap water
6 to 8 washers
empty prescription medicine container, large enough for the washers to fit in
24-inch (60-cm) pieces of string
¼ cup (60 ml) cooking oil
small bowl

PROCEDURE

1. Fill the glass three-fourths full with water.

2. Place 2 or 3 washers in the container and tie the ends of the strings around the top of the container. Tie the other ends of the strings together to form a loop.

3. Place the container in the glass of water and support it upright by holding the loop.

4. Continue to add washers until the top of the container is just below the surface of the water. Remove the container and pour out any water, but keep the washers inside.

5. Pour the oil into the glass, then slowly lower the weighted container into the glass.

6. With the loop, support the container so that its top is just below the surface of the oil.

7. When the container fills, raise it, pour its liquid contents into the bowl, and observe the liquid.

8. Continue to fill the container until all the oil is removed from the glass.

RESULTS The first few collections are pure oil, then a mixture of oil and water is collected.

WHY? Oil is a very visible pollutant (something that makes a substance dirty or impure) of the oceans. Because it floats and does not mix with seawater, it can be retrieved more easily than other pollutants. One method of retrieval is very similar to this method. An oil drum is weighted so that its top is just beneath the surface. The floating oil flows into the drum and is then pumped out.

FLOATER

PURPOSE To demonstrate the position of an iceberg in water.

MATERIALS 3-ounce (90-ml) paper cup
tap water
large-mouthed quart (liter) jar

PROCEDURE

1. Fill the cup with water.

2. Place the cup in the freezer for 2 hours or until the water in the cup is completely frozen.

3. Fill the jar three-fourths full with water.

4. Remove the ice from the cup. To do this, wrap your hands around the cup for 5 to 6 seconds. The warmth from your hands will melt some of the ice, making it easy to remove from the cup.

5. Tilt the jar and slowly slide the ice into the jar.

6. Observe the amount of ice above and below the surface of the water.

RESULTS More ice is below the water's surface than above it.

WHY? When water freezes, it expands. Thus the density of ice is slightly less than the density of water. As a result, ice is lighter than water and it floats. Icebergs, like the cup of ice, also float in water. Like all floating ice, most of the iceberg is below the water's surface.

BULGING BALL

PURPOSE To determine why Earth bulges at the equator.

MATERIALS construction paper—16 inches (40 cm) long
scissors
paper glue
paper hole punch
ruler
pencil

PROCEDURE

1. Measure and cut 2 separate strips, 1¼ inch x 16 inches (3 cm x 40 cm), from construction paper.

2. Cross the strips at their centers and glue.

3. Bring the four ends together, overlap, and glue, forming a sphere.

4. Allow the glue to dry.

5. Cut a hole through the center of the overlapped ends with the hole punch.

6. Push about 2 inches (5 cm) of the pencil through the hole.

7. Hold the pencil between your palms.

8. Move your hands back and forth to make the paper sphere spin.

RESULTS While the sphere is spinning, the top and bottom of the strips flatten slightly, and the center bulges.

WHY? The spinning sphere has a force that tends to move the paper strips outward, causing the top and bottom to flatten. Earth, like all rotating spheres, bulges at the center and has some flattening at the poles. The difference between the distance around Earth at the equator and the distance around Earth at the poles is 42 miles (67.2 km).

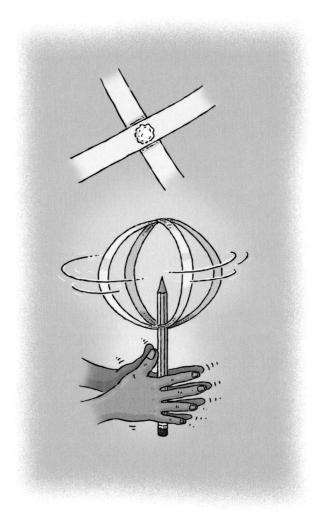

PRECESSION

PURPOSE To demonstrate the movement of Earth's axis.

MATERIALS modeling clay
round toothpick

PROCEDURE

1. Shape a piece of clay into a ball about the size of a marble.

2. Push the toothpick through the center of the clay ball so that just the tip of the pick sticks out one side.

3. Place the tip of the toothpick on a table.

4. Twirl the long end of the pick with your fingers.

5. Observe the movement of the top of the toothpick.

NOTE: The ball spins poorly if the toothpick is not through the center or if the clay is not round.

RESULTS As the clay ball spins, the top of the toothpick moves in a circular path.

WHY? As the ball spins, there is a shifting of the weight because the ball is not perfectly round. Earth, like the clay ball, wobbles as it rotates because of the slight bulge at the equator. Earth's axis (the imaginary line through the poles of Earth) moves in a circular path as Earth wobbles. This movement is called precession. The top of the toothpick makes many revolutions as the clay ball spins, but it takes 26,000 years for Earth to wobble enough for its axis to make one complete turn.

WOBBLER

PURPOSE To demonstrate how the composition of Earth affects its motion.

MATERIALS marking pen
1 hard-boiled egg
1 raw egg
CAUTION: Have an adult hard boil the egg.

CAUTION: Always wash your hands after touching an uncooked egg. It may contain harmful bacteria.

PROCEDURE

1. Allow the boiled and raw eggs to stand at room temperature for about 20 minutes.

2. Mark numbers on each egg—boiled: 1; raw: 2.

3. Place both eggs on a table, and try to spin each egg on its side.

RESULTS The hard-boiled egg spins easily and continues to spin for a few seconds. The raw egg wobbles and stops more quickly than the cooked egg.

WHY? The material inside each shell affects the way it spins. The cooked egg has a solid content that spins with the shell. The liquid inside the raw egg does not start spinning with the movement of its shell. The outer shell motion does cause the liquid to move, but slowly. The sluggish movement of the liquid causes the egg to wobble and stop more quickly. Parts of Earth's mantle and outer core are liquid. Earth's interior is not solid, and like the egg, Earth wobbles during its rotations. Unlike the egg's wobbling, Earth's wobbling is very slight and takes many years for a noticeable change.

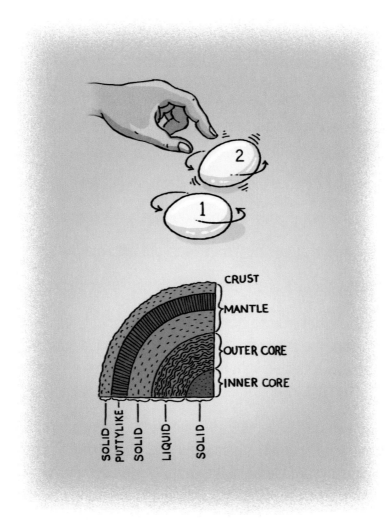

CRUST
MANTLE
OUTER CORE
INNER CORE

SOLID
PUTTYLIKE
SOLID
LIQUID
SOLID

DAY AND NIGHT

PURPOSE To determine the cause of the day and night cycle.

MATERIALS table
flashlight
dark shirt
small hand mirror

NOTE: This experiment needs to be performed at night.

PROCEDURE

1. Place the flashlight on a table and turn it on. The flashlight is to be the only light source in the room.

2. Stand about 12 inches (30 cm) from the flashlight wearing a dark shirt.

3. Slowly turn toward your left until you face away from the flashlight.

4. Hold the mirror at an angle to reflect light onto the front of your shirt.

5. Complete your turn and observe the front of your shirt as you turn.

RESULTS A spot of light moves across your shirt toward your right side as you face the flashlight. Your shirt is dark when you turn away from the light until the reflected light from the mirror shines on the shirt. The reflected light is not as bright as the light directly from the flashlight.

WHY? Your shirt represents Earth, the mirror the moon, and the flashlight the sun. Your turning imitates the rotation of Earth on its axis. As Earth turns toward the east, the light from the sun moves across the rotating Earth. Daytime is experienced by the people on the side facing the sun, and reflected light from the moon brightens the side of Earth that's turned away from the sun. The nighttime is very dark when the moon is not in position to reflect the sun's light onto Earth.

TWILIGHT

PURPOSE To determine why the sky is not dark as soon as the sun sinks below the horizon.

MATERIALS

quart (liter) jar	eyedropper
shoe box	spoon
milk	scissors
flashlight	adult helper

PROCEDURE

1. Fill the jar with water.

2. Add one drop of milk to the water and stir.

3. Ask an adult to cut a hole in the bottom of a shoe box next to the end. The hole should be round and large enough for the jar to fit in.

4. Turn the box upside down and ask an adult to cut a hole in the box's side large enough to fit the flashlight.

5. In a darkened room, turn the flashlight on and place it through the hole in the side of the box.

6. Stand the jar of water in the hole in the upturned bottom of the box.

RESULTS The water in the jar above the surface of the box has a pale blue-gray appearance.

WHY? Light is composed of different waves of color. When blended together, they appear as white light. Each wave of colored light is a different size. The larger waves pass through the glass unaffected by the small particles of milk throughout the water. Blue light waves are small enough to be scattered by the milk particles. Some of the scattered light enters the water in the upper section of the glass, causing it to have a bluish-gray color. Twilight is the time just after the sun sinks below the horizon. The sky is not dark at twilight because the light from the sun, like the light from the flashlight, is scattered by dust particles and gas molecules in Earth's atmosphere.

SALTY

PURPOSE To determine how salt beds are formed.

MATERIALS glass bowl, 2 quarts (2 liter)
measuring cup, 1 cup (250 ml)
measuring spoon, tablespoon (15 ml)
table salt

PROCEDURE

1. Stir together in the bowl 1 cup (250 ml) of water and 4 tablespoons (60 ml) of salt.

2. Allow the bowl to sit undisturbed until all the water evaporates. This may take 3 to 4 weeks.

RESULTS Cubic crystals line the bottom of the bowl, with white frosty deposits on the inner sides of the bowl.

WHY? Beds of salt are believed to have formed from shallow ponds that were close enough to the ocean to collect salt water and were then cut off from the sea. Slow evaporation of the water in the pond, as in the bowl, left behind clear cubic salt crystals called halite. Climbing clumps of frosty salt are formed where water rises up the sides of the pond or container, and salt in the solution crystallizes as the water quickly evaporates. This fast drying does not allow the salt molecules to move into position to form cubic crystals. The random depositing of the salt molecules produces the frosty crystals.

GLOSSARY

CENTRIFUGAL FORCE Outward force exerted by an object moving in a curved path.

COMPRESS To push together.

CONDENSE To change from a gas into a liquid.

CREST The highest part of a wave.

DENSITY The scientific way of comparing the "heaviness" of materials.

DEW Water droplets formed when atmospheric moisture condenses.

DEW POINT The temperature at which dew forms.

DOWNDRAFT Sinking air.

EVAPORATE To change from liquid to a gas.

GRAVITY The force that pulls toward the center of a celestial body, such as what occurs on Earth.

HIGH TIDE The point of greatest rise or bulging of the ocean.

MOLECULE The smallest particle of a substance; made of one or more atoms.

POLLUTANT Something that makes a substance dirty or impure.

RADIATE To move away from; movement of heat away from a warm object.

REVOLUTION Movement around a central point, as Earth moves around the sun.

ROTATE To spin on one's axis.

SEA BREEZE Air moving from the sea toward the land.

THUNDER Sound waves produced by the fast expansion and contraction of air molecules around lightning.

TORNADO A violently rotating funnel cloud that touches the ground.

TRANSVERSE WAVE Waves that move material up and down or side to side as the energy of the wave moves forward.

TROUGH The lowest part of a wave.

UPDRAFT Rising air.

VORTEX The funnel shape of a tornado; a whirling mass of air or water.

FOR MORE INFORMATION

Canadian Federation of Earth Sciences (CFES)
Department of Earth Sciences
FSS Hall
Room 15025
Ottawa, ON K1N 6N5
Canada
(902) 697-7425
Website: http://www.cfes-fcst.ca
The CFES is a federation of earth science member societies throughout Canada. Read about careers, get your earth science questions answered by an expert with the Ask a Geoscientist! tool, or use their Earth Links to find a multitude of resources about earth science.

National Aeronautics and Space Administration (NASA)
Ames Earth Science Division
NASA Headquarters
300 E Street SW, Suite 5R30
Washington, DC 20546
(202) 358-0001
Website: http://geo.arc.nasa.gov
NASA is the premier organization for all things about space and planet Earth! Join the NASA Kids' Club, see photos of Earth from space, and learn more about earth science research.

National Center for Earth and Space Science Education (NCESSE)
PO Box 2350
Ellicott City, MD 21041-2350
(301) 395-0770

Website: http://ncesse.org
The NCESSE creates and oversees national programs addressing STEM education, with a focus on Earth and space. Check out their links to Family Science Night, contests, experiment programs, and other community events.

National Geographic Society
1145 17th Street NW
Washington, DC 20036
Museum (202) 857-7700
Website: http://www.nationalgeographic.com
The National Geographic Society has been inspiring people to care about the planet since 1888. It is one of the largest nonprofit scientific and educational institutions in the world. Read their *Kids* magazine, enter the National Geographic Bee, or visit the museum.

National Science Foundation (NSF)
4201 Wilson Boulevard
Arlington, VA 22230
(703) 292-5111
Website: http://www.nsf.gov
The NSF is dedicated to science, engineering, and education. Learn how to be a Citizen Scientist, read about the latest scientific discoveries, and find out about the newest innovations in technology.

Society for Science and the Public
Student Science
1719 N Street NW
Washington, DC 20036

(800) 552-4412

Website: http://student.societyforscience.org

The Society for Science and the Public presents many science resources, such as science news for students, the latest updates on the Intel Science Talent Search and the Intel International Science and Engineering Fair, and information about cool jobs and doing science.

US Geological Survey (USGS)

12201 Sunrise Valley Drive

Reston, VA 20192

(888) 275-8747

Website: http://www.usgs.gov

The USGS collects, monitors, analyzes, and provides scientific data about natural resource conditions, issues, and problems on Earth. Check out their aerial and satellite images, use their many educational resources, or Ask a Librarian to help with your earth science questions.

WEBSITES Due to the changing nature of internet links, Rosen Publishing has developed an online list of websites related to the subject of this book. This site is updated regularly. Please use this link to access this list: http://www.rosenlinks.com/JVCW/earth

FOR FURTHER READING

Ardley, Neil. *101 Great Science Experiments*. New York, NY: DK Ltd., 2014.

Ball, Nate. *The Science Unfair*. New York, NY: Harper, 2014.

Buczynski, Sandy. *Designing a Winning Science Fair Project*. Ann Arbor, MI: Cherry Lake Publishing, 2014.

Candlewick Press. *Ruff Ruffman's 44 Favorite Science Activities*. Somerville, MA: Candlewick Press, 2015.

Dickmann, Nancy. *Exploring Planet Earth and the Moon*. New York, NY: Rosen Publishing, 2016.

Garbe, Suzanne. *Living Earth: Exploring Life on Earth with Science Projects*. North Mankato, MN: Capstone Press, 2016.

Harris, Tim, ed. *Earth Science*. New York, NY: Cavendish Square, 2016.

Hyde, Natalie. *Earthquakes, Eruptions, and Other Events that Change Earth*. New York, NY: Crabtree Publishing Co., 2016.

Katirgis, Jane. *Eerie Earthquakes*. New York, NY: Enslow Publishing, Inc., 2016.

Latta, Sara. *All About Earth: Exploring the Planet with Science Projects*. North Mankato, MN: Capstone Press, 2016.

McGill, Jordan. *Earth Science Fair Projects*. New York, NY: AV2 by Weigl, 2012.

Shea, Therese. *Freaky Weather Stories*. New York, NY: Gareth Stevens Publishing, 2016.

Sneideman, Joshua. *Climate Change: Discover How It Impacts Spaceship Earth*. Whiter River Junction, VT: Nomad Press, 2015.

Sohn, Emily. *Experiments in Earth Science and Weather*. North Mankato, MN: Capstone Press, 2016.

Sohn, Emily. *Experiments in Earth Science and Weather with Toys and Everyday Stuff*. North Mankato, MN: Capstone Press, 2016.

INDEX

A
air movement, 10–11, 12–13
air volume, 8–9
atmospheric temperature, 16–17

B
buoyancy, 42–43

C
centrifugal force, 38–39

D
dew point, 20

E
Earth
    atmosphere, 52–53
    axis, 46–47, 50–51
    composition of, 48–49
    high tides, 38–39
    motion of, 48–49
    poles, 45
    rotation of, 44–45, 46–47, 48–49
equator, 44–45, 46

H
halite, 54
heat energy, 20–21

I
icebergs, 42–43

L
lightning, 25
light waves, 52–53

M
moon, 38–39

O
oceans
    effect of density on water
        movement, 28–29
    and pollutants, 40–41
    salt content of, 34, 36–37
    tides, 38–39
    waves, 26
oil, 40–41

P
pollutant, 40–41
precession, 46
pressure, 8–9, 32–33

R
rain gauge, 18–19

S

salt beds, 54–55
salt water, 28, 34–35, 36–37
sea breezes, 14–15
sodium chloride, 34
soil, 14, 36–37
sun, 17, 36, 20, 52–53

T

thunder, 24–25
tides, 38–39
tornado, 22–23
twilight, 52–53

V

volcanic clouds, 16–17
vortex, 23

W

water density, 28
water waves, 26